W. H. Gill

**The Bible Catechist**

W. H. Gill

**The Bible Catechist**

ISBN/EAN: 9783337172824

Printed in Europe, USA, Canada, Australia, Japan

Cover: Foto ©Lupo / pixelio.de

More available books at **www.hansebooks.com**

THE

# BIBLE CATECHIST

## AN INSTRUCTION

IN

## BIBLICAL INTRODUCTION FOR THE YOUNG

BY THE

R ev. W. H. GILL, D.D.

AUTHOR OF "THE TEMPLE OPENED"

PHILADELPHIA

PRESBYTERIAN BOARD OF **PUBLICATION**
AND SABBATH-SCHOOL WORK

No. 1334 CHESTNUT STREET

.

WESTCOTT & THOMSON,
*Stereotypers and Electrotypers, Philada.*

# PREFACE.

THIS little work is on the plan of the author's guide to the Book, "The Temple Opened," and is an instruction in Biblical introduction for the young. The favor with which the larger work has been received by the clergy and the laity alike, led the author to believe that a miniature work of the same character might prove useful as an aid in the religious education of the rising generation. In this judgment the Board of Publication has concurred, and hence the issue of the Catechist with its imprimatur.

The great importance of putting our youth in actual possession of such instruction as is herein contained, needs no emphasis at the hands of the author. This is conceded by all; and it only remains therefore with parents and religious educators in general to see that what is so essential shall be actually accomplished.

The Catechist has been prepared with reference to its use in the Sunday-school, both by the teacher in the class and by the superintendent in general Bible drills. Put a Catechist in the hands of each scholar, and, with ordinary diligence, its contents may be mastered in about a year, and thus be laid a solid foundation for a subsequent and intelligent study of the Book of books.

3

Though the Catechist is published by the Presbyterian Board, it can be safely used by any other denomination, as there is nothing sectarian taught in it. It contains only facts about the Bible and its books which every Christian should know.

The author has in preparation a Bible Primer, or a Catechism in Scripture history, which, while designed immediately for young children and primary classes, will be found, he hopes, to be of service to such adult persons as are not familiar with the truths taught therein.

W. H. G.

PHILADELPHIA, 1893.

# THE BIBLE CATECHIST.

## THE BIBLE AND OTHER SACRED BOOKS.

*1. What is the Bible?*

The book sacred to Christians, containing, as it does, the
spired records of the Christian religion.

*2. Why is this book, sacred to Christians, called the
'ible?*

It is so called by way of eminence, because it is the best
? books. The word *bible* means book; any book therefore
*a* bible, but the book sacred to Christians is called *the*
ible, because it is the Book of books.

*3. What are some of the other names by which this sacred
'lume is known?*

It is called "The Word," "The Word of God," "The
:riptures," "The Holy Scriptures," and "Holy Writ"—
tles which indicate its source and nature, and the rever-
ice due to the book as such.

*4. Is the Christian's Bible the only book in the world
garded as sacred?*

No; every false religion has its own bible or book, which
; devotees regard as sacred, even as Christians do theirs.

*5. What are the other prominent books of the world
hich are regarded as sacred?*

The Koran, the bible of the Mohammedans; the Zend-
vesta, the bible of the Persians; the Shasters and the
edas, the sacred books of India; the writings of Confu-
us and the books of Buddha, which are regarded as

5

sacred by the Chinese, Japanese and other Asiatics; and the book of Mormon in our own country.

*6. What is the radical difference between other so-called sacred books and our Bible?*

Our Bible is given by inspiration of God, and is therefore of divine origin and authority; while the so-called sacred books of other religions are uninspired—simply the product of the minds of the men who wrote them—and are therefore in themselves destitute of any divine authority or warrant. Our Bible is the one book which claims God as its author, unmixed truth for its contents and salvation for its end.

*7. How may the superiority of our Bible over the other so-called sacred books of the world be shown?*

By the men it makes, the character it produces, and the civilization it develops. Witness in these respects the vast difference between those people and countries where our Bible is supreme and those where the other so-called sacred books exercise dominion. Compare Europe with Asia, or North America with South America. By its fruits the Bible is known, as is every tree.

*8. What authority do Protestants ascribe to the Bible?*

The supreme authority in morals and religion, in Church and in State. To them the Bible, and the Bible alone, is the only infallible rule of faith and practice.

*9. Why do Protestants accord to the Bible this supreme authority?*

Because it is the Word of God. To them, in and through it, God speaks, making known his will; its authority therefore is to them the authority of God, as its voice to them is the voice of God.

## THE BIBLE AS A BOOK.

*10. What is peculiar about the Bible as a book?*

It is not a single book or volume, but a collection of vol-

umes—a library, in fact, composed of *sixty-six* volumes—
embracing almost every variety of literature—biography,
history, poetry, law, letters, political economy, military
annals, morals and theology. The early Christians spoke
of the various parts of the sacred volume as "The Books,"
and it was not till the thirteenth century that the whole
came to be called, as it now is, "The Bible."

*11. Were the books of the Bible written at one time, or at
long intervals; by one person, or by many authors?*

They were not written at one time nor by one person, like
other so-called sacred books, but are the product of at least
forty different authors who lived at periods very remote
from each other, the length of time embraced in their composition being about sixteen hundred years.

*12. How does the Bible compare with other books as to
age?*

If we except the literature of ancient Egypt and Assyria,
portions of which are being uncovered by modern explora-
tions, the Bible contains in the books of Job and of Moses,
if not the oldest, certainly among the most ancient extant
literary compositions in the world.

*13. Were the books of the Bible always divided into chap-
ters and verses as they are now?*

No; such division is of comparatively recent date, and is
wholly without inspired authority or warrant; and, while in
many respects exceedingly useful, as it not infrequently
obscures the sense it should be ignored in the reading and
study of the Word.

*14. In what languages were the books of the Bible origi-
nally written?*

The Old Testament books were originally almost wholly
written in Hebrew; while those of the New Testament
were entirely in Greek.

*15. When and by whom were the books of the Bible first
translated into English?*

By Wyckliffe, about five hundred years ago—one hundred years before the discovery of America, and before the invention of printing. The first printed edition of the Bible in English was published by Tyndale more than one hundred years later, in the early years of the second quarter of the sixteenth century (1526–32).

*16. When and by whom was the version of the Bible in common use translated into English?*

Between the years 1607 and 1611, by men appointed for the purpose by James I. of England; whence it is commonly called King James' Version.

*17. Has there been any other version of the Bible made since that of King James?*

Yes; there is what is known as the Revised Version, which was made by representative biblical scholars of England and America, and published, the New Testament in 1880, and the Old Testament five years later, in 1885. This version, though most excellent in many respects and of great value as an aid to the meaning of the sacred text, has not become a favorite with the common people.

## HISTORIES IN THE BIBLE.

*18. What, in a word, is the great subject of the Bible?*

Redemption, the divine method of the salvation of sinful man. As a whole the sacred volume may best be described as a History (containing the inspired records) of Redemption.

*19. What special histories are embraced in this History of Redemption?*

The history of the whole race from Adam to Abraham (universal history) during a period of two thousand years; the history of the Jews, the descendants of Abraham, during a period of fifteen hundred years; the history of the Redeemer, our Lord and Saviour Jesus Christ, embracing His life of thirty-three years; and the history of the apostolic era, or the planting of the Christian Church in the world, covering the last two-thirds of the first Christian century;—the pre-Abrahamic or universal history; the history of the Jews; the history of the Redeemer ; and the history of the planting of the Christian Church.

*20. In what portion of the sacred volume are these histories respectively to be found ?*

The pre-Abrahamic or universal history is to be found in the first eleven chapters of Genesis ; the history of the Jews, Abraham's descendants, embraces all the remaining parts (nearly the whole) of the Old Testament; the history of the Redeemer is to be found in the Gospels; and that of the planting of the Christian Church in the world, in the Acts and Epistles.

*21. Why is so large a part of the Bible taken up with a history of the Jews, Abraham's descendants ?*

Because, as our Lord said to the woman of Samaria (John 4 : 22), "Salvation is of the Jews." By them the knowledge of JEHOVAH, the one living and true God, was preserved in the world, and of them, as concerning His human nature, our Redeemer, Christ, came. For this purpose they were raised up and chosen of God.

*22. Who was Abraham ?*

The father of the chosen people, and the head of the great spiritual household of faith—"the father of all them that believe" of all peoples and races.

*23. What are the three names, in their historical order, by which Abraham and his descendants are known ?*

They were known first as Hebrews—that is, immigrants, the people from beyond the river, the river Euphrates, where was Abraham's native home; second, as Israelites, the covenant name of the chosen people, so called from Jacob, the grandson of Abraham, whose name was changed to Israel, "a prince of God," and who was the father of the "twelve tribes" of which the Israelitish nation was composed; and third, as Jews, the name by which all the surviving descendants of Jacob have been commonly known (irrespective of their tribal relations) since their return from the Babylonian exile—Hebrews, Israelites, and Jews.

## THE BIBLE IN ITS PARTS.

*24. What do the Scriptures principally teach ?*

What man is to believe concerning God, and what duty God requires of man; that is, faith and works, or doctrine and duty.

*25. What is the honor due respectively to the written and the incarnate Word ?*

As the voice of God speaking to man, we bow to the authority of the one; while as God manifest in the flesh, we worship the other.

*26. What are the two grand divisions of the Bible ?*

The Old and the New Testament; that is to say, these two grand divisions contain the inspired records of God's former method and present plan of dispensing the grace of salvation to sinful men.

*27. What are the great dispensations under which God has been pleased to convey the grace of salvation to sinful men ?*

There are three: the Patriarchal, the Mosaic, and the Christian dispensation.

## THE OLD TESTAMENT.

*28. What is the nature of the Old Testament division of the Bible ?*

It contains the literature of the Hebrew people—the inspired records of the Israelitish nation, the channel of salvation to the Gentile world.

*29. Of how many separate books is the Old Testament composed ?*

In our English Bibles, thirty-nine; in the Hebrew, however, being divided differently, the number is not so great. These thirty-nine books constitute the sacred library of Old Testament literature.

*30. How are these thirty-nine Old Testament books commonly grouped or classified?*

Under four heads, called respectively the Pentateuch, the Historical, the Poetical and the Prophetical division.

*31. How many of the thirty-nine books are contained in each of these divisions?*

In the Pentateuch, 5; in the Historical division, 12; in the Poetical, 5; and in the Prophetical, 17.

## THE PENTATEUCH.

*32. Why is the first division of the Old Testament called the Pentateuch?*

The word itself is composed of two Greek words which mean *five books*, and the first five books of the Old Testament are called the Pentateuch, or the *five-volumed* book, called by the Jews the *Thorah* or the Law, because so large a part of the books is taken up with the laws and institutions to which they owed their existence as a nation.

*33. Who was the writer of the Pentateuch?*

It has been the common belief of the Church, Jewish and Christian alike, that Moses was the inspired author of this part of the sacred volume.

*34. What do we learn from the Pentateuch concerning the Hebrew people?*

It tells us of their origin, growth and organization into a nation, and of their history as a people during the first forty years of their existence as an organized body.

*35. What was the peculiar form of the government of the Hebrew people?*

It was a theocracy—the form of government in which JEHOVAH himself was at once Sovereign, Lawgiver and divine Administrator, carrying on His operations through persons and agencies chosen by Himself. In these respects the Hebrew people differed from all the other nations of the earth.

*36. Has the theocracy become extinct in the earth ?*

No ; though the Hebrew people have no longer an existence as a nation, the Christian Church is the successor of ancient Israel, and its members, in so far as they are truly Christian, are the theocratic people of this era.

*37. What are the names by which the Pentateuchal books are commonly known ?*

Genesis, Exodus, Leviticus, Numbers and Deuteronomy.

### GENESIS.

*38. Why is the first book of the Bible and of the Pentateuch called Genesis ?*

Genesis means *origin*, the beginning of anything; and Genesis is the book of origins, the beginnings of all things.

*39. Is the name Genesis sufficiently broad to cover the contents of the entire book ?*

No ; the title only properly applies to the story of the Creation, while all the rest of the book is the history, outcome or development of the things brought into being during the creative week.

*40. What is the scope of the history in Genesis ?*

While it is universal in its character up to the calling of Abraham, embracing a fragmentary account of the entire human family for two thousand years, from this point it narrows down and confines itself to the history of this illustrious patriarch and his immediate descendants during a period of some three hundred and fifty years. The universal history is but an introduction to and preparation for the particular or theocratic history which follows.

*41. How, according to its contents, may the first fifth of the Pentateuch be fitly designated ?*

It may be called Genesis; or, the book of the Patriarchs, the ancestors of the Hebrew people. Hence in Genesis we have the origin of the elect nation.

*42. What was the distinguishing characteristic of the dispensation inaugurated in Abraham?*

Separation; he was to leave his country and kindred, that he might become the father of a mighty race, which was in turn to be a "holy nation," the "peculiar people" of God.

*43. How long is the dispensation inaugurated in Abraham designed to last?*

To the end of the world, the consummation of all things, when the final and complete separation shall take place between the righteous and the wicked at the judgment of the great day.

*44. Into how many eras may this great Abrahamic age be divided?*

Three : the Patriarchal era, or that of the separate family; the National era, or the period of the separate Hebrew people; and the Christian era, or the times of the Gentiles, the period of the separate Church. The Family, the Nation, the Church—these are the three great eras of the Abrahamic age.

*45. Which of these eras falls within the scope of Genesis?*

The Patriarchal, which begins with the call of Abraham, and ends with the death of Joseph—a period of about three hundred and fifty years.

*46. At what time did the call of Abraham take place?*

About the year of the world 2000; that is, at a point midway between Adam and Christ; about the same length of time before Christ as has now elapsed since His advent.

*47. Where do we find the posterity of Abraham at the close of Genesis?*

In Egypt, where, according to the plan of God, they were to become a great nation.

*48. How many did Abraham's descendants number when they went down to Egypt, and who were they?*

Seventy souls in all—viz. : Jacob and his twelve sons and their children. Neither their wives nor their servants are reckoned in the number.

*49. What are the names of the twelve sons of Jacob?*

Reuben, Simeon, Levi and Judah, Issachar and Zebulun (sons of Leah); Dan and Naphtali (sons of Zilpah, Leah's maid); Gad and Asher (sons of Bilhah, Rachel's maid); and Joseph and Benjamin (the sons which Jacob's beloved wife Rachel bore to him). These twelve sons of Jacob are the twelve patriarchs whence sprung the twelve-tribed nation, the Israelitish people, the Jews.

*50. Through which of these twelve sons of Jacob was the promised Seed, the Christ, to come?*

Judah, the fourth son. The line of descent was thus : Abraham, Isaac, Jacob, Judah.

*51. What period of time is covered by the book of Genesis?*

About 2350 years. Thus, at the close of only the first book of the sixty-six of which the sacred volume is composed we are more than half-way through the Bible in point of time. For from the creation of Adam to the death of Joseph in Egypt there are considerably more than 2000 years; and from Moses to John in Patmos, who wrote the last book of the New Testament, there are as many years less than 2000 as there are more than that number covered by the book of Genesis; that is, nearly 400 years.

*52. Who are the three leading characters in the book of Genesis?*

Adam, the first head of the human family; Noah, the second head of the race ; and Abraham, the father of the Hebrew people and the head of the great spiritual household of faith.

*53. To what class of literature does Genesis as a book belong ?*

History; that is, the contents of the book are historical; but they are history in the form of biography, by far the larger number of events recorded in the book having individuals for their centre. Genesis may therefore be said to be a book of biography.

*54. What are the great pivotal events in the book of Genesis, in their historical order ?*

The Creation, the Fall, the Flood, the Confusion of Tongues, the Calling of Abraham, the Birth of Isaac the child of promise, and the Descent of Jacob and his family, Abraham's descendants, into Egypt.

## EXODUS.

*55. How does Genesis as a book compare with Exodus ?*

Because of the fullness and richness of its contents Genesis may truly be said to be a wonderful book; while Exodus, because of the peculiar nature of its contents, may as truly be said to be a book of wonders. It is full of the supernatural—no other book is more so.

*56. How may Exodus itself as a book be described ?*

As pre-eminently the book of God—JEHOVAH. From beginning to end His voice is heard, His hand is seen, His person is manifested. It contains more august divine disclosures or visible manifestations of deity than any other of the books which compose the Old Testament.

*57. What great truth concerning JEHOVAH do the contents of Exodus demonstrate ?*

His universal sovereignty and supremacy over all that is called God. The sovereignty of JEHOVAH, and JEHOVAH as Sovereign—these two points cover the contents of this second fifth of the Pentateuch.

*58. In what peculiar character does God manifest Himself to His own people in Exodus ?*

In Genesis God had made Himself known to the patriarchs as Father and Friend, Protector and Guide; but in Exodus He reveals Himself to His people as Redeemer and Saviour. In Genesis He appears as the great Promiser; in Exodus He is seen as Jehovah, the great Performer—the covenant-keeping God.

*59. Why is the book of Exodus so called?*

Exodus means a going out or departure, and the book is so called because it contains an account of the wondrous deliverance of the children of Israel from the land of Egypt.

*60. Is Exodus a title sufficiently comprehensive to cover the whole contents of the book?*

No; like Genesis, it is too narrow, covering, as it does, only the first half of the contents of the book; and, the second part being so unlike the first, it is difficult, if not impossible, to find any single term to embrace the whole.

*61. What is the nature of the contents of Exodus?*

The first part is wholly historical, while the second part is about equally divided between that which is historical and that which is apocalyptic; that is, between that which recounts the doings of the people and that which records the sayings or revelations of Jehovah Himself.

*62. What is the central point in the book of Exodus?*

Mount Sinai in Arabia, the point to which God led the children of Israel after their deliverance from Egypt, and the scene of the giving of the law. Indeed, Sinai may be regarded as the central point of the entire Pentateuch. All that precedes leads up to it and is a preparation for it, while all that follows is but the outcome of what there took place.

*63. What is the difference between the condition in which we leave the Israelites in Genesis and that in which we find them in Exodus?*

In Genesis we leave them in prosperity and honor; in Exodus, 150 years later, we find them in a state of galling servitude. Entering the south country as princes, they became slaves; the land of Egypt became to them a house of bondage.

*64. How was the deliverance of the children of Israel from the Egyptian bondage effected?*

By the direct interposition of God JEHOVAH in their behalf, Who, through the agency of His servant Moses, whom He raised up and qualified for the purpose, by a series of plagues, ten in number, compelled the unwilling monarch Pharaoh to let His people go.

*65. What were the Ten Plagues of Egypt?*

Turning the water into blood; frogs; lice; flies; murrain of cattle; boils; fire and hail; locusts; darkness; and the last and most terrible, the death of all the first-born of man and beast in all the houses of the Egyptians.

*66. What religious ordinance was instituted in connection with the Exodus?*

The Passover. By direction of God the Hebrew people in their respective families slew a lamb, whose blood was sprinkled on the door-posts and lintels as a sign to the destroying angel, when going on his errand of death, to pass over those houses whereon was this evidence of faith and obedience. The ordinance which was thus instituted as a means of the salvation of Israel was to be annually observed as a memorial of the event throughout all their future generations.

*67. How did JEHOVAH conduct His people out of Egypt?*

He went before them in a pillar of cloud by day, and by night in a pillar of fire, to lead them in the way.

*68. What was the final act by which the deliverance of the Hebrew people from the bondage of Egypt was completed?*

The dividing of the Red Sea, through which the Hebrew people passed on dry ground; and the which, when the Egyptians essayed to do, they were drowned.

2

*69. What did the people of Israel do after they thus saw their deliverance so wonderfully effected?*

They sang the song of Moses on the other side of the sea, after their passage through the water. In this song is extolled the triumph of JEHOVAH over their former masters and pursuers, the Egyptians.

*70. Whence did JEHOVAH lead His emancipated people after the triumphant passage of the Red Sea?*

Through the wilderness to Mount Sinai, which place they reached after a journey or march of about two months.

*71. What were the leading events which took place at Sinai, as recorded in Exodus?*

The giving of the Moral Law—the Ten Commandments; the giving of the code of laws which, together with the Decalogue, composed the National Covenant, the compact between JEHOVAH and the Hebrew people; the solemn inauguration of the Covenant, and the tabernacle revelation. The first part of Exodus is historical; its middle part is legislative; and its latter half is institutional—pertaining to the tabernacle and its services.

*72. What sad incident marred the proceedings at Sinai?*

The worship of the golden calf, and the breaking of the two tables of the law by Moses, which he cast upon the ground in an outburst of indignation at this sign of apostasy on the part of his people. This lapse on the part of the people, with its sad consequences, and their restoration to the divine favor, and how it was effected, are recorded in chapters 32–34 inclusive.

*73. How often and how long was Moses in the mount with God?*

Twice; each time extending over a period of forty days and nights, and during which seasons he neither ate nor drank.

*74. Under what general headings may the contents of Exodus be grouped?*

Three : Israel in Egypt ; from Egypt to Sinai ; and the transactions at Sinai.

75. *What sub-title, in addition to its present name, would best indicate the contents of Exodus?*

Owing to the central place the national compact occupies among the events in the book, it might be called Exodus ; or, the Book of the Covenant. The National Covenant : its nature ; the parties to it ; the time when, the place where, and the circumstances under which it was entered into, together with the obligations and privileges which either accompany or flow from it. This subject thus distributed would suggest and cover the entire contents of this second fifth of the Pentateuch.

## THE TABERNACLE.

76. *What was the tabernacle?*

It was the tent or place of meeting between God and His people—at once the palace or earthly dwelling-place of JEHOVAH and the sanctuary for His worship.

77. *What were the three grand divisions of the tabernacle?*

The outer court, the holy place, and the innermost sanctuary or the holy of holies.

78. *What was the furniture of these divisions of the tabernacle respectively?*

In the outer court were the brazen altar and the brazen laver, the altar of sacrifice for the people, and the place of purification for the priests ; in the holy place were the table of shew-bread, the golden candlestick, and the altar of incense or golden altar ; and in the most holy place the ark of the covenant, the mercy-seat, and the cherubim which sat upon it.

79. *What sacred deposit was placed in the ark of the covenant?*

The two tables of the law, and probably Aaron's rod that budded, and the pot of manna.

*80. What are the three arks of Scripture?*

Noah's ark, the ark in which the child Moses was laid,
and the ark of the covenant.

*81. Who were the officers in charge of the tabernacle and
its services?*

The priests, the sons of Aaron, and the Levites, all of
whom were members of the tribe of Levi, Jacob's third
son, who were set apart by direction of God for this service. These were ministers of state as well as officers of
religion.

## LEVITICUS.

*82. What is the nature of this third fifth of the Penta-
teuch?*

It is the priestly book, containing the ritual of the Hebrew
religion. As the book of the covenant in Exodus contained
the civil statutes and judgments by which the elect people
were to be guided in their internal affairs and external relations, so the religious laws and institutions given here in
Leviticus supply what was yet wanting for their complete
equipment as the people of God. Leviticus, which contains the ceremonial law, may therefore be described as the
book of ceremonies or directory of worship of the Hebrew
people.

*83. Who prescribed these rites and ceremonies of the He-
brew religion?*

JEHOVAH Himself. Hence, almost the entire book of
Leviticus is made up of the very words of the supreme
Law-giver Himself, Moses being only the mediator and
promulgator thereof.

*84. Were the laws in Leviticus delivered from the same
place as those of Exodus?*

No; the ceremonial enactments in Leviticus were given,
as was fit, from the tabernacle, the tent of propitiation itself,
at the foot of Mount Sinai, by God, as Saviour; while the

civil legislation of Exodus was given from the top of the mount by God JEHOVAH as sovereign.

85. *What is a brief outline of the contents of Leviticus?*

It contains the laws of sacrifice; the laws to be observed by the priests and Levites, both as to their consecration and their official duties; sanitary laws; the ceremonies to be observed in connection with the great Day of Atonement; the fixing of the sacred times of Israel; and other minor and miscellaneous matters.

86. *What is the central chapter and subject in Leviticus?*

The sixteenth chapter, which treats of the great Day of Atonement. Than this there is no more significant chapter or subject in all the Old Testament, clearly prefiguring, as it does, our Lord's death and resurrection, and His appearance meantime in the presence of God for us. The great Day of Atonement was to the Hebrew people what crucifixion day and its sequel are to the Gentile world.

87. *What were the chief annual festivals of the Hebrew people?*

The Passover, which commemorated the deliverance from Egypt; Pentecost, or the Feast of 'Weeks (occurring seven weeks after the Passover), or the festival of the First-Fruits; and the Feast of Tabernacles and Ingathering, or the Harvest Home, the closing festival of the Jewish year. At each ot these three annual feasts all male persons over twelve years were required to appear before JEHOVAH.

88. *Is Leviticus an evangelical book?*

Yes; it is full of the truth that sanctifies and saves. All its sacrifices point forward to the one great sacrifice. In fact, it may with great propriety be called "The Gospel according to Leviticus." It has been pronounced "the clearest book of Jewish gospel."

89. *What book in the New Testament is the key to Leviticus?*

The Epistle to the Hebrews. In this book, whose great

theme is the priesthood of Christ, it is clearly seen how the rites and services of the Levitical economy point to Him as their antetype and fulfillment.

*90. What are the key-thoughts of Leviticus?*

Sacrifice and sanctification; or, the way to God and the walk with God.

## NUMBERS.

*91. Why is this fourth fifth of the Pentateuch called Numbers?*

It is so called from the twofold occurrence of the making up the muster-roll of those capable of bearing arms and amenable to military duty—the first when the people were about to start off upon their march to the land of promise, and the second at the end of the forty years in the wilderness. Like the titles of the previous portions of the Pentateuch, "Numbers" is by no means a sufficient index to the contents of the entire book.

*92. What is the nature and scope of the contents of this book of Numbers?*

The history contained in it is of a military character, and it gives an account of the marshaling of the people according to their tribes, of their march from Sinai to the borders of the promised land, and of the conquest of the territory on the east side of Jordan.

*93. How long did the children of Israel linger about Mount Sinai?*

About one year, during which time the laws of Exodus were given, the tabernacle constructed and erected and the laws of Leviticus dictated to Moses.

*94. What are the chief incidents in the story of the march from Sinai to Canaan as recorded in Numbers?*

The celebration of the Passover before starting out; the giving of the people quails for food; the sedition of Miriam and Aaron and its punishment; the report of the spies and

the people's rebellion in consequence thereof, and its punishment; the stoning of the Sabbath-breaker; the rebellion
of Korah and his company, and its punishment; the bring-
ing of water out of the rock at Meribah; the death of Miriam
and Aaron, and the appointment of Aaron's successor; the
story of the brazen serpent; the victory over Sihon and
Og; the story of Balaam; the spoiling of the Midianites;
and the appointment of Joshua as Moses' successor.

*95. What is a peculiar feature in the contents of the book
of Numbers?*

The alternation of laws, enacted as the emergency arose,
with the historical narrations. There is a great variety of
such legislation scattered through this long book.

*96. For what is Numbers as a book remarkable?*

The signal display of God's judgments against sin with
which the account abounds; and this not merely in the case
of the heathen, as Sihon and Og, but toward His own people,
not even Moses and Aaron escaping the consequences of their
unfortunate misdemeanors.

*97. What are the chief lessons of the book of Numbers?*

It teaches the sin and evil of unbelief, and that warfare
is the necessary condition of pilgrimage and possession.

*98. What were the results to the children of Israel of their
wilderness experience?*

It gave to them their national unity, their laws and institutions, individual liberty, military discipline, and religious
education.

*99. What is a brief summary of the book of Numbers?*

Forty years of Moses; or, the Failures and Successes of
the Church Militant—the Church in the wilderness.

## DEUTERONOMY.

*100. Why is this last fifth of the Pentateuch called Deu-
teronomy?*

The word itself means the "second law" or the repetition

of the law, and the book doubtless takes its name from the fact that so large a part of it is taken up with the substantial reproduction of the laws of Exodus. The title, however, is inadequate, seeing that it neither correctly expresses the nature, nor covers the whole, of the contents of the book.

*101. What then is the nature of this book of Deuteronomy, and how may it be expressed?*

The book is sermonic rather than legislative in its character, and may be described as the Lawgiver's Appeal; or, Moses' Farewell Address to his Countrymen.

*102. What is the object of this farewell address of Moses to his countrymen?*

To impress upon the people a sense of their obligation to JEHOVAH their God, Who had so wondrously redeemed them, and to urge upon them the duty of obedience to His law and faithfulness to His covenant.

*103. How does Moses, as preacher, proceed in effecting his object in this farewell address?*

He first recounts their history, then recalls their laws, and finally reminds the people of the solemn compact or covenant into which they had entered with JEHOVAH at Sinai, soon after their deliverance from the bondage of Egypt. This address, which is divided into these three sections, takes up the first thirty chapters of the book.

*104. What are the other chief matters contained in the remaining part of this book of Deuteronomy?*

Moses' charge to Joshua, his dying song, and his blessing the twelve tribes as Jacob had blessed the heads thereof; the account of his death and burial; the whole being concluded with a brief eulogy of the great lawgiver.

*105. What service did this book of Deuteronomy render to our Lord?*

He found in it the arrows with which He repelled the assaults of Satan in His temptation in the wilderness.

*106. What is the great lesson Moses endeavored to impress upon his people in the book of Deuteronomy?*

It is that obedience is the condition of the divine favor and of the permanent possession of the promised land.

*107. What period of time is embraced in the pentateuchal story?*

From the creation of Adam to the death of Moses—according to the common chronology, about 2500 years.

## THE HISTORICAL BOOKS.

*108. How many and what are the books of the historical division of the Old Testament?*

They are *twelve* in number as they stand in our English Bible : Joshua, Judges, and Ruth ; the three doubles—the Samuels, the Kings, and the Chronicles ; Ezra, Nehemiah, and Esther.

*109. Are not the pentateuchal books historical, as well as those distinctively so called?*

Yes; in the broadest sense they are so ; but because so large a portion of the Pentateuch is taken up with their laws and institutions, the Hebrew people designated that division of their Scriptures as the *Thorah;* that is, the Law.

*110. Of what are these twelve books the history?*

Of the Hebrew people as an organized body. In the Pentateuch we have an account of the origin, growth, and organization of the Hebrew people into a nation ; and in these twelve books we have the history of the nation in outline from the death of Moses, its founder, to Malachi, the last of the prophets—a period of about 1100 years.

*111. Into how many periods may the history of the Hebrew people as a nation be divided?*

Three : the period of the Theocracy, the period of the Monarchy, and the period of the Restoration.

## THE THEOCRACY.

*112. What period is embraced by the theocracy distinctively so called?*

The interval between Moses and the monarchy; that is, between the death of the nation's founder and the appointment of Saul as king—a period of about 400 years.

*113. What was the distinctive feature of this theocratic period in the history of the Hebrew people?*

The direction of affairs of state was lodged solely in the hands of JEHOVAH Himself.

*114. How many and what are the books which treat of the theocracy?*

Three: Joshua, Judges, and Ruth.

*115. What is the nature of the book of Joshua?*

It is a military history, which gives an account of the conquest and division of the land of promise under Joshua, the hero of the story. The book reads like *Grant's Memoirs* or *Cæsar's Commentaries.*

*116. Who succeeded Joshua?*

He had no successor: by his death the nation was left without any visible head or federal authority, the twelve tribes preserving their independence in the management of their own internal affairs.

*117. What, during this period, was the centre of national unity for the twelve tribes?*

The tabernacle, the place of meeting between the people and God. They were bound together by the double tie of race and religion.

*118. How is the period immediately succeeding the administration of Joshua known?*

As the period of the Judges—a class of men whom God raised up from time to time to deliver the people from the enemies He allowed to oppress them because of their apostasy from, and disloyalty to, Himself.

*119. How many judges were there, and what are the names of the chief ones among them ?*

There were fifteen in all, the chief of whom were Deborah and Barak, Gideon, Jephthah, Samson, Eli, and Samuel.

*120. Where do we find an account of the period of the judges ?*

In the books of Judges, Ruth, and the early part of first Samuel.

*121. What is the nature of the book of Ruth ?*

It is a simple and beautiful love-story of rural domestic life, being an incident which took place in the days when the judges ruled, and in which Ruth and Naomi are the leading characters. A story of filial love and moral purity, it flashes like a star in the midnight of its dark surroundings.

*122. How is this period of the theocracy commonly characterized ?*

As the Iron Age of Israel; as the period of David and Solomon is called its Golden Age.

## THE MONARCHY.

*123. What books treat of the monarchical period of Hebrew history ?*

The three doubles—the Samuels, the Kings, and the Chronicles. Herein we have the history of the rise, culmination, division, decline, and fall of the Hebrew monarchy.

*124. How long did the Hebrew monarchy last ?*

From its foundation in Saul till the captivity of Judah— about 500 years.

*125. How long did the united kingdom last ?*

During the reigns of Saul, David, and Solomon (each of whom reigned 40 years)—120 years.

*126. What became of Solomon's empire ?*

Under Rehoboam, Solomon's son and successor, the Ten Tribes revolted from his rule and founded the kingdom of

Israel; while the two tribes of Judah and Benjamin adhered to the house of David, constituting the kingdom of Judah. Thus Solomon's empire was divided, forming two independent realms and rival kingdoms—Israel and Judah.

*127. How long did these two rival kingdoms stand?*

Israel, the northern kingdom, stood a little over two centuries and a half (254 years), and had nineteen kings; while Judah survived its northern rival 134 years, lasting nearly 400 (exactly 388) years, and had twenty kings. Unlike those of Israel, these were all of the house of David.

*128. What became of these two kingdoms, Israel and Judah?*

They were both destroyed by peoples of the East; Israel or the Ten Tribes being first carried away captive into Assyria, and subsequently the people of Judah into Babylon. The latter, however, after their seventy years' captivity in Babylon, returned in large numbers to their own land and re-established the religion of their fathers, while the Ten Tribes never recovered their national existence, and are commonly regarded as lost.

*129. What are the contents of the two books of Samuel?*

The first, after detailing the events in the history of the last two judges, Eli and Samuel, gives an account of the rise and inauguration of the monarchy in Saul, and of his reign of forty years; while the second is wholly taken up with the splendid reign of David, the hero-king of Israel. The names of these two books are misleading, being not at all an index to the nature of their contents.

*130. What are the contents of the two books of Kings?*

Taking up the story of the monarchy with the last days of David, these two books carry the history down to the Babylonian captivity—from Solomon to Zedekiah king of Judah—a period of about 400 years.

*131. How do the two books of Chronicles differ from the two books of Kings?*

Besides giving the genealogy of the Hebrew people from Adam down to David, the "Chronicles" are mainly concerned with the history of Judah; while in the Kings the history of both kingdoms is given. Chronicles, as far as the southern kingdom is concerned, is parallel with the history in Kings.

*132. What great event brought the Hebrew monarchy to a close?*

The destruction of Jerusalem and the captivity of the people of Judah by Nebuchadnezzar, king of Babylon.

*133. How long did the Babylonian exile last?*

The prophetic seventy years, after which, in the providence of God, the people of the captivity, as many as chose, were permitted to return to their own land. Only a small fraction, however, of the number who were carried away captive, or their children, availed themselves of this permission to return.

*134. Where do we learn of the condition of the Hebrew people during their Babylonian exile?*

There are no historical books specially devoted to this period, and such information as is available must be gathered from the prophets of the period, the books of the restoration, and the Psalms of the exile.

### THE RESTORATION ERA.

*135. What is meant by the era of the Restoration?*

It designates that period in the history of the Hebrew people immediately succeeding the Babylonian exile, when the Jewish captives returned to their own land and rebuilt the temple and re-established on its old foundations the religion of their fathers. From this time onward the people first known as Hebrews, and then as Israelites, become known as Jews.

*136. What books treat of this restoration era?*

The last historical triplet—Ezra, Nehemiah, and Esther.

*137. Who were the leading characters of the restoration era ?*

Joshua and Zerubbabel, Ezra and Nehemiah, and Haggai and Zechariah; the first pair being the ecclesiastical and civil leaders of the first band of returning captives; the second pair, the leaders of the second and third bands; and the last two being the prophets who co-operated with Joshua and Zerubbabel in the rebuilding of the second, commonly called Zerubbabel's, temple.

*138. Who were the prophets of the restoration era ?*

Haggai, Zechariah, and Malachi, the last named being contemporary with, and the coadjutor of, the last historical character of Old Testament story—Nehemiah.

*139. Of what do the books of Ezra and Nehemiah respectively treat ?*

Each has a story to tell of return, rebuilding, and reformation. The first tells of the return of the first band of captives and the rebuilding of the temple, and of the return of Ezra with his company and the reforms which he wrought; while the second tells of the return of Nehemiah, the rebuilding of the walls of Jerusalem, and the reformations which he succeeded in effecting.

*140. What is noteworthy about Nehemiah as a book ?*

It is the last historical book in the Hebrew Scriptures. With it closes the Old Testament Canon; the book of Esther, which follows, being but an episode which took place in the time of Ezra; just as the book of Ruth contains the account of an incident which took place in the days when the judges ruled in Israel.

*141. What is the nature of the book of Esther ?*

It is a story of providence and patriotism, in which Esther, a Jewess and the beautiful queen of the Persian monarch, risks her own life for the salvation of her people, a plot for whose utter extermination was foiled through her efforts.

*142. What is remarkable about this book of Esther?*

Though a romance of providence, the name of God is not in it. The same is true of Canticles, or the Song of Solomon.

*143. Who are the leading characters in this book of Esther?*

The king Ahasuerus (who was Xerxes), Esther the queen, Mordecai the Jew, and Haman the Agagite, the Jews' enemy.

*144. What are the four " sevens" mentioned in this book of Esther?*

The seven days of the royal feast to the people ; the seven chamberlains of the king ; the seven princes of Persia ; and the seven maidens of Esther.

*145. Who are the five persons whose names begin with H, mentioned in this book of Esther?*

Hadassah (who is Esther) ; Hege, the king's chamberlain and keeper of the harem ; Hatach, also one of the king's chamberlains and minister-in-waiting upon the queen ; Haman the Agagite, the Jews' enemy ; and Harbonah, the king's chamberlain, who counseled the hanging of Haman.

*146. What are the names of the two leading characters in the story of Esther which begin with M?*

Memucan, one of the seven princes of Persia and counselor to the king ; and Mordecai the Jew.

*147. What are the three pairs in Esther?*

Two queens, Vashti and Esther ; two rivals, Mordecai and Haman ; and two would-be regicides or assassins of the king, Bigthana and Teresh, the king's chamberlains.

*148. What became of the rivals, Mordecai and Haman?*

Haman was hanged on the gallows which he himself had erected, and on which he expected to hang Mordecai, whom through envy he hated ; while Mordecai was promoted to the high place in the king's service to which Haman had been exalted.

*149. What period of time is included in the restoration era?*

From the proclamation of Cyrus, giving permission for the exiles to return, to the close of the Old Testament Canon (Nehemiah–Malachi)—nearly, but not quite, 150 years.

## THE POETICAL BOOKS.

*150. How many and what are the poetical books of the Old Testament?*

There are five books commonly reckoned in this division, namely: Job, Psalms, Proverbs, Ecclesiastes, and Canticles, or the "Song of Songs, which is Solomon's." "Lamentations," one of the most poetical of compositions, now classed among the prophetical books, might very properly have found a place in this division.

*151. Why is the book of Job so called?*

It is so called from Job, the patriarch of Uz, who is the hero of the poem.

*152. Who are the dramatis personæ—the leading characters—in the book of Job?*

The Lord JEHOVAH, the moral governor of the universe; Job himself, a rich man, perfect and upright; the patriarch's three friends, Eliphaz the Temanite, Bildad the Shuhite, and Zophar the Naamathite; then there is also the young orator Elihu the Buzite; and Job's wife, who has obtained an unenviable notoriety as the bad adviser of her husband by the utterance of a single sentence.

*153. What is the great problem to be solved in the book of Job?*

Whether there is such a thing as disinterested rectitude among men, or whether they are selfish and mercenary in their loyalty to God, serving Him only so long as, and because, it pays to do so. Satan charged that the latter was the fact, alleging that the piety of good men is only assumed.

*154. How alone could such a problem as this be solved?*

By actual experiment, putting some one to the test. Job in this case was the subject of the experiment, Satan being allowed of God to put him to the severest tests that even his malignant ingenuity could devise. This poem might therefore be very appropriately entitled "The Temptation of Job," even as the ordeal to which our Lord was subjected by the same adversary in the wilderness is called "The Temptation of CHRIST;" and, indeed, the former is typical of the latter.

*155. What erroneous theory of God's government obtained in Job's day?*

That prosperity was the reward bestowed upon goodness, and that adversity was a sure sign of wickedness, either concealed or manifest. Hence men concluded that because Job was a great sufferer he was therefore a great sinner. This, indeed, was Job's own theory, and it added greatly to his perplexity and to the intensity of his suffering that he was unable, the while, to reconcile his afflictions with his conscious integrity.

*156. How did Job stand his trial?*

Though not without occasional and violent outbursts of impatience, yet he maintained his integrity to the end, so that when he was tried he came forth as gold. Thus Satan's allegation was proved false. The patriarch of Uz was not mercenary in his motives in serving God.

*157. With what other Old Testament worthies does God link the name of Job?*

With those of Noah and Daniel. The order in which they are mentioned is Noah, Daniel, and Job (Ez. 14 : 14, 20).

*158. What are the triplets in the book of Job itself?*

There are the three friends of Job—Eliphaz, Bildad, and Zophar; the three animals of Job—the Arabian war-horse, the behemoth, and the leviathan; the three daughters of Job—Jemima, Kezia, and Karen-happuch.

*159. To what may the book of Job be likened?*

To a gymnasium, the exercising ground for the development of spiritual athletes, or to a furnace in which metals are assayed or tested.

*160. What is the nature of the book of Psalms?*

It is a collection of sacred odes, one hundred and fifty in number, and which constitutes the Praise-Book not only of the Jewish Church, but also of some sections of the Christian Church (Presbyterian) as well. It is called the Hebrew Psalter, as modern praise-books are called church hymnals.

*161. What is the difference between the Psalms and other parts of Holy Scripture?*

The Psalms are purely devotional in character. In other parts of Scripture God speaks to man, but in the Psalms man speaks to God. The Psalms are the outgrowth of human experience.

*162. When and by whom were these Psalms composed?*

The Psalms were composed by various authors and at different eras from Moses down to the Restoration, covering a period of more than a thousand years. The Psalter is thus a book of long growth, and is made up of five different volumes, which may be called the Psalter Nos. 1, 2, 3, 4, and 5, very much as our "Gospel Hymn" books have grown and are so named.

*163. Why are these songs of Zion commonly called the "Psalms of David"?*

Not because David was the author of all, but because he was, in all probability, the largest contributor to, and editor of, the original collection, Psalter No. 1 ; and as each new collection was added to the first volume, the whole came to be called by the name of the "sweet singer of Israel," and to be commonly known as the Psalms of David.

*164. To what may the book of Psalms be likened?*

To a conservatory of music where dwell all the sons and

daughters of song, with cymbal, trumpet, psaltery, and harp.

165. *To what may the book of Proverbs be compared?*

To a "Chamber of Commerce," where may be found that ancient "wealth of nations" whence every human mind may enrich itself with the wisdom of the ages. If the book is not a rule of faith, it most certainly is a rule of conduct for both sexes and for all ages and conditions.

166. *What are the chief subjects touched upon in this book of Proverbs?*

They are such as filial piety, evil company, sensuality and drunkenness, lying and laziness, strife and greed.

167. *Who is the author of the book of Proverbs?*

The book is of composite authorship, like the Psalms, but it is ascribed to Solomon, the "Grand Monarque" of Israel, for the same reason that the Psalms are to his royal father—he being doubtless the largest contributor to the collection of proverbs therein contained.

168. *To what may the book of Ecclesiastes be compared?*

To the penitentiary, where sorrowful bankrupts and other moral defaulters may remain for a time with profit in company with King Solomon, reflecting over the follies of a misspent life.

169. *To what conclusion does the preacher in Ecclesiastes come?*

That to fear God and keep His commandments is at once the highest wisdom, as it is the whole duty, of man.

170. *What is the key-word of Ecclesiastes?*

"Vanity"—which occurs twenty-five times in the course of the composition. "Vanity of vanities," saith the preacher—"Vanity of vanities; all is vanity."

171. *What warning does the preacher in Ecclesiastes administer to the fast young man?*

"Rejoice, O young man, in thy youth: and let thy heart cheer thee in the days of thy youth, and walk in the ways of thine heart, and in the sight of thine eyes: but know thou that for all these things God will bring thee into judgment."

*172. What good advice does the preacher in Ecclesiastes give to all young people?*

"Remember now thy Creator in the days of thy youth, while the evil days come not, nor the years draw nigh, when thou shalt say, I have no pleasure in them."

*173. What is the nature of Canticles, or the Song of Solomon?*

It is a dramatic love-song, consisting of a dialogue between two lovers—the exquisite celebration of a pure love in humble life—a love which no earthly splendor can dazzle and no flattery seduce. The piece is a protest against the harem.

*174. How do Christian interpreters look upon this song?*

Some of them regard it as a marriage-song and an allegory—a dialogue between the bridegroom and the bride, between CHRIST and His Church.

*175. To what do the Jews compare these three books of Solomon?*

To the temple—Proverbs to the outer court, Ecclesiastes to the holy place, and Canticles to the holy of holies.


## THE PROPHETICAL BOOKS.

*176. What is the scriptural idea of a prophet?*

Not a mere foreteller, as is the common idea, but rather a *forthteller*, one who speaks for, or is the authorized representative of, another.

*177. What were the Hebrew prophets?*

They were the representatives of JEHOVAH, the authorized and inspired expounders or interpreters of His will. The Hebrew prophets were, in fact, the preachers of their time, predictions being only an incidental function of their office ; and the prophetical books contain the sermons of these inspired preachers.

*178. Were the Hebrew prophets limited to the male sex ?*

No ; Miriam, Deborah, and Huldah were shining lights in this goodly fellowship.

*179. What is the history of the prophetic order ?*

Its foundations were laid in Samuel, at the close of the theocracy; it flourished during the monarchy, and remained a power till the work of restoration was complete; after which, for 400 years, until the appearance of John the Baptizer, the forerunner of our Lord, the voice of the prophet was no longer heard in the land.

*180. How many prophets are represented by their sermons in the Old Testament Canon ?*

Sixteen : Isaiah, Jeremiah, Ezekiel, Daniel, Hosea, Joel, Amos, Obadiah, Jonah, Micah, Nahum, Habakkuk, Zephaniah, Haggai, Zechariah, and Malachi.

*181. Are there more prophetical books than prophets in the Old Testament Canon?*

Yes; besides the book which bears his name, Jeremiah wrote Lamentations also, making *seventeen* sermon-books or books of prophecy, and but *sixteen* prophets or preachers in this division of the Old Testament Scriptures.

*182. When did these canonical prophets flourish ?*

Beginning with Jeroboam II. of Israel, about 800 B. C., they flourished during the last half of the monarchical period, during the time of the Babylonian captivity, and on to the close of the restoration era, covering a period of some 400 years.

*183. Into what three classes may these sixteen canonical prophets be divided ?*

Accordingly as they lived before, during, or after the Babylonian captivity—which is the great epoch in the later Hebrew history, to which every event is referred—they may be regarded as pre-exile prophets, prophets of the exile (captivity), and post-exile prophets, or the prophets of the restoration.

*184. Which were the prophets of the restoration ?*

The last three in the list—Haggai, Zechariah, and Malachi.

*185. Which were the prophets of the exile ?*

These were two, Ezekiel and Daniel, both of whom spoke and wrote in Babylon.

*186. How many and which were the pre-exile prophets ?*

There were *eleven :* Isaiah, Jeremiah, Hosea, Joel, Amos, Obadiah, Jonah, Micah, Nahum, Habakkuk, and Zephaniah.

*187. What is an easy way to ascertain the names of the pre-exile prophets ?*

Cut off from the list the last three, the prophets of the restoration, strike out Ezekiel and Daniel, the prophets of the captivity, and the remaining eleven are the pre-exile prophets. Some think that Obadiah lived during the exile, though his prophecy is directed against Edom, with only an incidental allusion to the future of his own people.

*188. How are the prophetical books divided as regards their length ?*

Into two classes—*major* and *minor ;* the first *five* books being reckoned as major, and the remaining *twelve* as minor.

*189. What are the names of the books which compose the Major Prophets ?*

Isaiah, Jeremiah, Lamentations, Ezekiel, and Daniel.

*190. What are the names of the twelve Minor Prophets?*

Hosea, Joel, Amos, Obadiah, Jonah, Micah, Nahum, Habakkuk, Zephaniah, Haggai, Zechariah, Malachi.

*191. Whence do these prophetical books derive their names ?*

They are called by the names of their authors respectively, except "Lamentations," which takes its name from the nature of the contents of that book, being a wail of

Jeremiah the prophet over the desolation of the holy city Jerusalem after its destruction by Nebuchadnezzar. The book of Lamentations is, in its truest sense, a jeremiad.

*192. What two famous prophets of Israel are not represented in the Old Testament Canon?*

Elijah and Elisha. These flourished in Israel at an earlier period than the canonical prophets, and are more famous for their deeds than their words. They were *acting* rather than *writing* prophets.

*193. How may the substance of the canonical prophecies be briefly expressed?*

By the three alliteratives: ruin, repentance, restoration.

*194. What two institutions date their origin from the period of the restoration?*

The synagogue, the local religious meeting-house of the Jews, and the order of Scribes, of both of which Ezra was the founder.

*195. What was the political status of the Jewish people during the 400 years' interval between Malachi and Matthew?*

They were successively tributary to the Persians, Greeks, Syrians, and Romans, save the century or so of independence they achieved and maintained under the heroic lead of the Asmoneans or Maccabean princes. They were under the dominion of Rome when CHRIST came.

*196. What important event affecting the Hebrew Scriptures took place between Malachi and Matthew?*

They were translated into Greek, as is commonly supposed by seventy persons; whence the name of the version, the Septuagint or the LXX. This translation was necessary to meet the want of the Jews of the Dispersion, who had now entirely ceased to speak the Hebrew language. Though the origin of this oldest version of the Hebrew Scriptures is shrouded in the deepest obscurity, it must have been in existence between two and three centuries before CHRIST. It was from this Septuagint version of the Old Testament Scriptures that CHRIST and his apostles most frequently quoted.

*197. What sects with which we meet in the New Testament grew up during this 400 years' interval?*

The Scribes, the Pharisees, the Sadducees, and the Herodians.

*198. What are the various periods in Old Testament story?*

The Antediluvian period, from the Creation to the Flood —1656 years; from the Flood to the call of Abraham—400 years; from the call of Abraham to Moses and the exodus from Egypt—400 years; from Moses to the monarchy, that is, the period of the theocracy—400 years; the monarchical period—500 years; the Babylonian captivity—70 years; from the captivity to the close of the restoration era—200 years; and from the close of the Old Testament Scriptures to CHRIST—400 years—all in round numbers.

*199. What is noteworthy about these chronological data?*

The predominance of the 400-year period in which God has been pleased to carry on the operations of His providence in the history of redemption. Nearly all these periods, if not exactly 400 years, are either a multiple of 400 or a fraction thereof. In addition to the other quarto-centenary periods already mentioned, the period during which the canonical prophets flourished was one of 400 years.

*200. Who are the epoch-making characters of the Old Testament period?*

Adam, Noah, Abraham, Moses, David, and Ezra.

## THE NEW TESTAMENT.

*201. What is the New Testament?*

The second grand division of the Bible, commonly called

the New Testament of our Lord and Saviour JESUS
CHRIST.

*202. Of what is the New Testament composed?*

Of *twenty-seven* distinct literary compositions commonly
called books. Like the Old Testament, which is composed
of *thirty-nine* books, it is a library of sacred literature rather
than a single volume.

*203. By whom were these twenty-seven books written?*

By at least eight different authors : thirteen by the apostle Paul ; five by the apostle John ; two by the apostle Peter ; two by the evangelist Luke ; one each by the evangelists Matthew and Mark ; and one each by the apostles
James and Jude. The authorship of the " Hebrews " is
in dispute, but it is commonly ascribed to Paul, which
makes his contribution to the New Testament fourteen
books.

*204. When were the books of the New Testament written?*

Unlike those of the Old Testament, whose writing ex-
tended over a period of more than 1000 years—from Moses
to Malachi—the books of the New Testament were all written during the last half of the first century of the Christian
era, and most of them during the third quarter of that century.

*205. What is the common classification of the books of the
New Testament?*

Like those of the Old Testament, they are commonly
grouped under four heads : the Gospels, the Acts, the
Epistles, and the book of Revelation.

*206. As to the character of their contents, how may these
four divisions be respectively described?*

The Gospels are biographic ; the Acts, historic ; the Epistles, didactic ; and the Revelation, apocalyptic.

*207. What are the names of the books of the New Testa-
ment?*

The four gospels—Matthew, Mark, Luke, and John ; the

Acts; the fourteen epistles of Paul the apostle—that to the Romans, the two to the Corinthians, the one each to the Galatians, Ephesians, Philippians, and Colossians, the two each to the Thessalonians and to Timothy, and the one each to Titus and Philemon, and that to the "Hebrews;" the seven non-Pauline espistles—the one of James, the two of Peter, the three of John, and the one of Jude; and the book of Revelation.

*208. What is the grand theme of the New Testament, and how are its various classes of books related thereto?*

The grand theme of the New Testament is the Christian Church; and the biographic gospels tell us of its Founder and Head, who is CHRIST; the historical book of the "Acts" tells us of its founding by the apostles; the didactic epistles contribute to its upbuilding or edification; while the book of Revelation opens up to us its future. The Christian Church: its Founder, its founding, its edification, its future.

*209. In what language were the books of the New Testament originally written?*

In Greek, the then universal language of the civilized world—a circumstance which emphasizes, as well as anything can, the universal or catholic design of the New Dispensation.

## THE FOURFOLD GOSPEL.

*210. What is the meaning of the word "gospel"?*

It means "good news" or "glad tidings;" and the four gospels are so called because they proclaim the advent of the Son of God for the salvation of sinners.

*211. What is the nature of the contents of these four gospels?*

They tell us all we know of the birth, life, and death of our Lord and Saviour JESUS CHRIST. They are biographical, while not pretending to be full and complete biographies. They are memoirs or memorabilia rather than biographics.

*212. In what character do the four evangelists respectively present JESUS?*

It is the supreme purpose of Matthew to set forth the messiahship of JESUS; that of Mark, the majesty of JESUS; that of Luke, the humanity of JESUS; and that of John, the godhood or divinity of JESUS.

*213. How do the first three gospels differ from the fourth?*

The first three, the "synoptics," as they are called, being an account mainly of what our Lord said and did, His miracles and teaching as He went about among the masses, are *about* CHRIST simply; while the fourth, the gospel according to John, reveals to us the interior life of our Lord, and brings before us CHRIST Himself. The contents of this gospel were addressed mainly to "the Jews"—that is, to the rulers of the people. It is pre-eminently the spiritual gospel—the heart of CHRIST.

*214. What are the characteristics of the four gospels respectively?*

The first is the gospel of discourses and of the parables of the kingdom; the second is anecdotal in its character, and, being composed largely of the miracles of our Lord, is the gospel of the mighty works; the third is distinguished by the fullness of its narratives of the infancy of JESUS and its wealth of parables; while the fourth is pre-eminently the gospel of conversations or dialogues.

*215. What are the key-words of the four gospels respectively?*

The key-word of Matthew is "fulfilled;" those of Mark, "straightway," "immediately," and "forthwith," the word in the Greek being the same for all three, and occurring *forty-five* times; those of Luke, "And it came to pass;" and those of John, "Verily, verily, I say unto you."

*216. What are the great facts, common to the four evangelists, which make the gospel good news to men?*

The incarnation, the life, the death, and the resurrection of our Lord.

*217. How many of our Lord's miracles and parables are recorded in the gospels?*

Thirty-six miracles and about thirty parables.

*218. How often did our Lord speak on the cross, and how many times did He appear after His resurrection?*

He uttered seven sayings on the cross, and appeared ten times after His resurrection.

*219. How many persons did our Lord raise from the dead?*

Three : Jairus' daughter; the son of the widow of Nain; and His friend Lazarus, the brother of Martha and Mary.

*220. How long did our Lord's public ministry last?*

Three years or about that time.

*221. What event in our Lord's history is common to all the evangelists?*

His passion. Nearly one-third of the entire gospels is taken up with the history of the last seven days of our Lord's life.

*222. What places were identified with the principal events in our Lord's life?*

Bethlehem, where He was born; Nazareth, where He was brought up; Capernaum, "His own city," where He dwelt during His public ministry; and Jerusalem, where He was crucified.

*223. How many times was our Lord put upon His trial?*

Five : before Annas, Caiaphas, and Pilate the first time; before Herod; and then before Pilate the second time, when He was delivered to be crucified.

*224. What length of time elapsed between our Lord's resurrection and ascension?*

Forty days, during which time He showed Himself alive to His apostles by many infallible proofs, and spoke to them of the things pertaining to the kingdom of God.

*225. What are the distinguishing characteristics of our Lord's teaching as exhibited in the gospels?*

Authority, originality, spirituality, tenderness, benevolence, and practicalness.

*226. What are the names of the twelve apostles?*

The three pairs of brothers—Peter and Andrew, the sons of Jonas; James and John, the sons of Zebedee; and James and Jude, the sons of Alpheus; Philip and Bartholomew; Thomas and Matthew; Simon the zealot; and Judas Iscariot, who also betrayed JESUS.

*227. What were the qualifications and functions of the apostles?*

The apostles were ambassadors extraordinary and ministers plenipotentiary of the LORD JESUS CHRIST, chosen and commissioned by Himself. They were inspired and endowed with the "gift of miracles." As preachers of the gospel the apostles were to be witnesses of CHRIST as to His doctrine, His manner of life, and especially of His death and resurrection. In their extraordinary functions the apostles had no successors.

## THE ACTS OF THE APOSTLES.

*228. What is the nature of the contents of the book called "The Acts of the Apostles"?*

It is the history of the Apostolic Church—of the founding or planting of the Christian Church in the world. It is the sequel to the third gospel, or volume the second of the evangelist Luke's history of the primitive Christian Church.

*229. What is the scope of this history of the Christian Church by Luke, as given in these two volumes?*

In it he traces the rise and growth of the Christian Church from the birth of its Founder and Head in the bosom of the Jewish Church to its complete emancipation from all Jewish trammels and its establishment among the

Gentiles, equipped for its work and secure of its mission, the conquest of the world.

*230. What was the supreme purpose of the evangelist in these two volumes, the gospel and the history?*

In the history it is manifestly the author's purpose to give a complete and precise view of that mighty religious revolution by which God transferred His kingdom from the Jews to the Gentiles; even as in the gospel it was his chief design to show how our Lord Himself was, by His crucifixion at the hands of His own people, emancipated from all Jewish restrictions to become the King of men, irrespective of race or nationality.

*231. What is the connecting-link between the two volumes, the gospel and the history?*

The ascension of our Lord. This event forms at once the climax of the history of the Church's Founder in the gospel and the starting-point for the history of the founding of the Church in the Acts. The goal in the one writing, it is the foundation of the other.

*232. Does this book contain the " acts " of all the apostles of our Lord?*

No; of the original twelve, only three, Peter, John, and James, are specially mentioned in the history as taking a prominent part in the "actings" it records; while Paul, the last chosen and commissioned apostle, who was as "one born out of due time," takes up a large share of the space in the interesting narration. The Acts is not designed to be a history of the apostles, but a record of the establishment of the Christian Church.

*233. What is the scope of the history in this book of the Acts?*

It recounts the story of the founding and extension of the Christian Church from Jerusalem, the ecclesiastical capital, to Rome, the political metropolis of the world. It begins with Pentecost, and ends with Paul a prisoner "in his own hired house " in the city of the Cæsars, " preaching the kingdom of God . . . with all confidence, no man forbidding him."

*234. How may the history in the Acts be divided?*

Into two parts : the first part detailing the history of the planting of the Church among the Jews, and the second part the planting of the Church among the Gentiles. The first part has the apostle Peter for its centre; the second, the apostle Paul. Around these two leading characters the entire history in the book is grouped.

*235. What was the point of transition in the passage of the Church from the Jews to the Gentiles?*

The vision of the apostle Peter on the house-top in Joppa, an account of which is given in the tenth chapter of this history.

*236. Who are the Gentiles?*

All that part of the entire population of the globe who are not Jews. Between these two peoples the entire human race is divided. All who are not Jews are Gentiles.

*237. What is the first great occurrence related in this history in the Acts?*

The descent of the HOLY SPIRIT at Pentecost, when three thousand souls were converted in one day.

*238. Who are the three persons in the Acts whose names begin with P?*

Peter and Paul, apostles, and Philip the evangelist.

*239. How may the relation of the apostles Peter and Paul to the Christian Church be expressed?*

Peter was the opener, and Paul was the planter—the first and grandest of Christian missionaries.

*240. Who were the first Christian martyrs according to this history in the Acts?*

Stephen the deacon was the first or proto-martyr, and the apostle James the second in this now glorious company.

*241. What tragedies are recorded in this history in the Acts?*

The death of Ananias and Sapphira the pretenders; the stoning of Stephen; the killing of James the apostle; and the death of the cruel and vainglorious Herod, who was eaten of worms and gave up the ghost.

*242. Are there any miracles recorded in this history in the Acts?*

Yes; twenty specific miracles of a physical character, two of which are the raising of the dead—Dorcas by the apostle Peter, and the young man Eutychus by the apostle Paul. By far the greatest miracle in the book, however—the one which has been attended with the most beneficent and far-reaching effects—was a miracle of grace, the conversion of Saul of Tarsus, who became the glorious Christian hero of this history—Paul, the great apostle of the Gentile world.

*243. How many capital cities are associated with the planting of the Christian Church, according to the history in the Acts?*

Four: Jerusalem, "the mother of us all;" Antioch in Syria, the mother church of Gentile Christendom; Ephesus in Asia Minor, the great religious and literary centre where Paul preached and John dwelt; and Rome in Italy, the city of the Cæsars, the political centre and capital of the then civilized world.

*244. To whose agency was the success of the efforts of the apostles in founding the Christian Church due?*

To that of the HOLY SPIRIT, the Third Person of the adorable Trinity, upon Whose co-operation we must still depend for every success in soul-winning and genuine Church extension.

## THE EPISTLES.

*245. What relation do the Epistles sustain to the "Acts"?*

The writing of these several letters was among the "acts

of the apostles," as they are themselves a part of the history of the founding and edification of the early Christian Church. The epistles bear the same relation to the history in the "Acts" that the books of prophecy in the Old Testament do to the historical books therein. They are mutually interpretative, each serving to throw light upon the other. This is more especially true of the Pauline epistles and the Acts.

*246. How many epistles compose this New Testament collection ?*

Twenty-one—the fourteen of the apostle Paul, being two-thirds of the whole number; the three of the apostle John; the two of the apostle Peter; and the one each of the apostles James and Jude.

*247. What is the common classification of these epistles ?*

They are commonly grouped under two heads—Pauline and catholic or general. Since, however, the latter term does not properly designate a number of the letters embraced under it, a more accurate classification is Pauline and non-Pauline.

## THE PAULINE EPISTLES.

*248. What are the names of the Pauline epistles ?*

They are those to the Romans, the Corinthians (2), the Galatians, the Ephesians, the Philippians, the Colossians, and the Thessalonians (2); and those to Timothy (2), Titus, Philemon, and the Hebrews. Nine are addressed to seven different Christian congregations, four to individuals, and one—that to the Hebrews—to the whole body of Jewish Christians wherever found.

*249. What are the epistles to Timothy and Titus commonly called ?*

The "pastoral epistles," for the reason that they are addressed to, and abound in practical counsels for, young ministers.

4

*250. What is the character of the other Pauline epistles?*

With the exception of that to Philemon, which is a letter of intercession in behalf of his runaway but penitent slave Onesimus, they are nearly all of a doctrinal character, but contain also practical instruction for the edification of the churches in general and their individual members in particular.

*251. What are the four dominant ideas of the Pauline epistles?*

Spirituality as opposed to ritualism or the mere ceremonies of religion; catholicity, or all humanity, as opposed to a particular people or a favored class; a pure life as over against mere orthodoxy; and personal attachment to JESUS CHRIST as the supreme motive to a pure life. These four ideas — spirituality, catholicity, a pure life, and JESUS CHRIST—are distinctively Pauline.

*252. What may be regarded as the golden text of the Pauline epistles?*

"God forbid that I should glory save in the cross of our LORD JESUS CHRIST, by Whom the world is crucified unto me, and I unto the world" (Gal. 6 : 14).

*253. What is the grandest generalization in the Pauline epistles?*

This: "In CHRIST JESUS neither circumcision availeth anything, nor uncircumcision, but a new creature; faith, which worketh by love, and the keeping of the commandments of God" (Gal. 6 : 15; 5 : 6; 1 Cor. 7 : 19).

*254. What is the most comprehensive exhortation in the Pauline epistles?*

This: "I beseech you therefore, brethren, by the mercies of God, that ye present your bodies a living sacrifice, holy, acceptable unto God, which is your reasonable service" (Rom. 12: 1).

*255. When were these Pauline epistles written?*

In the early part of the second half of the first Christian

century; that is, between A. D. 52 and A. D. 68, embracing a period of sixteen years.

## THE NON-PAULINE EPISTLES.

*256. How many and what are the non-Pauline epistles?*

They are seven in number, and, in the order in which they are found in the New Testament Canon, are as follows: the one of the apostle James, the two of the apostle Peter, the three of the apostle John, and that of the apostle Jude.

*257. What is the difference in the manner of naming the Pauline and non-Pauline epistles?*

The Pauline epistles are known by the names of the churches or the particular body of Christians to which they were addressed; while the non-Pauline epistles are known by the names of the persons by whom they were written.

*258. What other group of letters is there in the New Testament besides these twenty-one canonical epistles?*

There are the letters of the apostle John to the seven churches of Asia—the churches of Ephesus, Smyrna, Pergamos, Thyatira, Sardis, Philadelphia, and Laodicea (Rev. 2 : 3).

*259. How can it be made to appear that there are two letters to the Ephesians and two to the Hebrews in the New Testament?*

Besides the canonical epistle of the apostle Paul to the Ephesians, there is that of the apostle John in the book of Revelation to the same people; and in addition to the canonical epistle of the apostle Paul to the Hebrews, there is also the canonical epistle of the apostle James to the Twelve Tribes, which embraced the whole of the Hebrew people.

*260. How may the Epistle of James be described?*

As the letter of the apostle Paul to Philemon may be characterized as the looking-glass for the Christian gentleman, so this epistle of James may be described as the looking-glass of the believer—the touchstone of Christian character. James declaims with great energy on the glory of practical virtue, confining himself almost exclusively to an earnest insistence on Christian practice.

*261. What is the nature of the two epistles of the apostle Peter?*

The first abounds in incentives to Christian perseverance in view of impending trials and persecutions; while the second, which is the apostle's valedictory, is a warning against apostasy, the antidote for which is progressive piety and implicit trust in the Holy Scriptures.

*262. What are the five precious things of the apostle Peter?*

Faith itself; the trial of faith; the promises, which are exceeding great as well as precious; the blood of CHRIST with which we are redeemed; and CHRIST Himself, who is to the believer above all things precious.

*263. Does the apostle Peter speak or write as if he were pope?*

No; in no instance does he lay claim to any such primacy or ecclesiastical supremacy. On the contrary, in the Acts he appears as only a member of the first great council in Jerusalem, of which James was the moderator or presiding officer; while in his letters he writes to the "elders," exhorting them as one of themselves, being himself also "an elder." The apostle Peter was undoubtedly *primus inter pares*—the first among equals—but possessed no official superiority above his brethren.

*264. Of how many books of the New Testament was the apostle John the author?*

Five; besides these three epistles, he wrote also the fourth gospel and the Apocalypse or the Revelation—the last book of the Bible.

*265. What prominence did John have among the brethren of the apostolic college?*

He was the disciple whom JESUS loved, and he outlived all his brethren, so that his writings are the latest utterance of any inspired man. John was therefore the "apostle of completion." Peter was the opener, Paul the planter, and John the finisher.

266. *What is peculiar about these three epistles ascribed to the apostle John?*

Like "the Hebrews," they are anonymous, the name of the apostle nowhere appearing in any one of them. In other ways, however, it is known that the beloved disciple was their author.

267. *How does the writer describe himself in the second and third epistles?*

As "the elder," who, from his great age, character, and position, everybody was supposed to know. Thus John and Peter were both "elders."

268. *How does the first epistle of John differ from the other two?*

The first epistle of John is of the nature of a treatise or discourse on the doctrines and duties of Christianity; while the second and third epistles are personal letters, the former addressed to "the elect body and her children," and the latter to "the well-beloved Gaius," a benevolent gentleman whose hospitality to some Christian missionaries greatly endeared him to the "beloved disciple," and whose conduct therein the apostle warmly commends.

269. *What are the three favorite words of the apostle John which begin with L?*

Life, light, love.

270. *What are the three definitions of God peculiar to the apostle John?*

God is spirit; God is light; and God is love.

271. *What is the most characteristic word in the writings of the apostle John?*

Love; which occurs fifty times in his gospel, and forty-

five times in his first epistle.   Love God and be like Him—
this is the great idea of the beloved disciple.

*272.  What two persons whose names begin with D are
mentioned in the third Epistle of John?*

Diotrephes, "who loveth to have the prominence among
them," domineering, dictatorial, obstructive, and Demetrius
(not the silversmith of the Acts), the very opposite of Diotrephes the unlovely, a man famous for his generosity and
Christian consistency.   Diotrephes the apostle condemns;
Demetrius he commends.

*273.  What is the gist of the epistle of Jude?*

It is a bugle-blast against latitudinarianism, and, like
second Peter, a warning against apostasy.

*274.  In what respect does the epistle of Jude resemble the
second and third epistles of John?*

In respect of their length.   They are all three short, being
each composed of but one chapter.   They are the briefest
independent portions of the entire Bible.

### THE REVELATION.

*275.  By what name is the book which constitutes the fourth
division of the New Testament called?*

The Apocalypse; or, the Book of Revelation.

*276.  What is the character of this last book of the New
Testament?*

It is a book of wonders—a wonderful book.   It is also a
book of seals, even as it is in itself the great seal of the
completed volume of divine truth—the splendid dome of
the glorious temple of Holy Scripture.

*277.  What is the grand theme of the Apocalypse?*

The second advent of CHRIST.   There is one voice in all its
epistles, seals, trumpets, vials, plagues, and visions of glory
and joy—The Lord cometh!

*278. What is the one grand disclosure the Apocalypse makes?*

That of the final triumph of Christianity over all its enemies and opposers, and its termination in an endless period of glory and happiness.

*279. To what are the triumphs of the Christian Church due, according to the Apocalypse?*

The Blood. The book is bathed in and saturated with the Blood. In the midst of its most heavenly scenes it celebrates the atoning Blood. Saints sing and angels speak of redemption *through* the Blood, cleansing *in* the Blood, and victory *by* the Blood of the Lamb.

*280. What are the seven classes of people in the Apocalypse who are called blessed?*

The doers of the word, the dead in the Lord, the vigilant, the marriage guests, those who have part in the first resurrection, the keeper of the sayings of the prophecy of this book, and they that, doing His commandments, wash their robes—these are called blessed.

*281. How many kinds of horses are there in the Apocalypse?*

Four : the white horse of victory, the red horse of war, the black horse of mourning, and the pale horse of devastation and death.

*282. What is the favorite title by which our Lord is designated in the Revelation?*

The same by which He was first pointed out to the multitude by His forerunner upon His entrance upon His public ministry—"The Lamb of God." From the beginning to the end, throughout the long conflict and in the midst of the glorious issue, there is still the one title for Him Who conquers and judges and reigns—"The Lamb."

*283. What are the terms in which the grand final gospel invitation of the Bible is couched?*

These: "And the SPIRIT and the Bride say, Come. And

let him that heareth say, Come. And let him that is athirst come. And WHOSOEVER will, let him take the Water of Life FREELY."

## SUPPLEMENTARY.

*284. Who are the leading human personages in Genesis?*

Adam, Noah, Abraham, Isaac, Jacob, and Joseph.

*285. Who is the leading human character in the last four books of the Pentateuch?*

Moses, the deliverer, the lawgiver, and the founder of the Hebrew commonwealth.

*286. Which is distinctively the law book of the Pentateuch?*

Exodus; therein is contained the Moral Law or the Ten • Commandments, and the National Covenant, that code of laws designed for the special government of the Hebrew people.

*287. Which are the two books of the Bible called after women?*

Ruth and Esther.

*288. In what two books of the Bible is the name of God not found?*

Canticles (the Song of Solomon) and Esther.

*289. What are the fifteen pairs of Genesis?*

The first pair—Adam and Eve; the two trees of the garden—the tree of knowledge of good and evil and the tree of life; the first murderer and his victim—Cain and Abel; the two lines from Adam to Noah—the Cainites and the Sethites; the two wives of Lamech the Cainite—Adah and Zillah; the two sons of Adah—Jabal and Jubal; the two children of Zillah—Tubal-cain and Naamah his sister; the two sons of Abraham—Isaac and Ishmael; the two cities of the plain destroyed by fire from heaven—Sodom and Gomorrah; the names of the two sons of Lot's two daugh-

ters—Moab and Ammon; the twin sons of Isaac and Re-
bekah—Jacob and Esau; the .twin sons of Tamar the
ancestress of our Lord—Pharez and Zarah; the two wives
of Jacob—Rachel and Leah; and his two concubines—Bilhah and Zilpah; the two sons of Rachel—Joseph and Benjamin; and the two sons of Joseph—Ephraim and Man-
asseh.

*290. What are the seven pairs of Exodus?*

The two treasure cities built for Pharaoh by the children
of Israel—Pithon and Raamses; the two God-fearing mid-
wives who saved the men children of the Hebrews alive,
contrary to the commandment of the king—Shiprah and
Puah; the father and mother of Moses—Amram and Jo-
chebed; the two sons of Moses—Gershom and Eliezer; the
brother and sister of Moses—Aaron and Miriam; the two
aids of Moses—Aaron and Hur; the two kinds of food
furnished the Israelites in the wilderness—quails and
manna.

*291. What are the three pairs of Leviticus?*

The two sons of Aaron who were slain for sacrilege—
Nadab and Abihu; the two substitutes for these slain
priests—Eleazar and Ithamar; the two pallbearers of Nadab and Abihu—Mishael and Elzaphan.

*292. What are the three pairs of Numbers?*

The two courageous spies—Caleb and Joshua; the two
kings whom Moses slew on his way to Canaan—Sihon, king
of the Amorites, and Og, king of Bashan; the prince of
Israel and the Midianitish woman who were slain for adul-
tery—Zimri and Cozbi.

*293. What is the one pair of Deuteronomy?*

Gerizim and Ebal—the mount of blessing and the mount
of cursing. ·

*294. What are the four pairs of Judges?*

The two heroines—Deborah the prophetess and Jael the
slayer of Sisera; the two princes of Midian whom the

Ephraimites slew—Oreb and Zeeb; the two kings of Midian whom Gideon slew—Zebah and Zalmunna; the two judges famous for their large families—Ibzan, who had thirty sons and as many daughters, and Abdon, who had forty sons and thirty nephews.

295. *What are the two pairs of Ruth?*

The two sons of Naomi—Mahlon and Chilion; and her two daughters-in-law—Orpah and Ruth.

296. *What are the seven pairs of the two Samuels?*

The father and mother of Samuel—Elkanah and Hannah; the two wicked sons of Eli the priest—Hophni and Phineas; the two degenerate sons of Samuel—Joel and Abijah; the Damon and Pythias of the Bible—David and Jonathan; the two assassins of Ishbosheth, Saul's son—Rechab and Baanah; the two men in whose houses the ark of God dwelt—Abinadab and Obed-edom; the two men who drove the cart on which the ark was put to be carried to Jerusalem —Uzzah and Ahio.

297. *What are the six pairs of the two Kings?*

The two men whom Solomon put to death on his accession to the throne—Joab and Shimei; the two kingdoms into which the empire of Solomon was divided—Israel and Judah; the two centres of worship which Jeroboam, the first king of Israel, designed to be rivals of Jerusalem— Bethel (in the south) and Dan (in the north); the two tribes which remained loyal to the house of David—Judah and Benjamin; the two great miracle-working prophets of Israel—Elijah and Elisha; the two persons who were raised from the dead—the son of the widow of Zarephath (by Elijah) and the son of the Shunammite (by Elisha).

298. *What are the two pairs of Ezra?*

Zerubbabel, the builder of the second temple, and Ezra, the scribe and religious reformer; and the prophets Haggai and Zechariah, who aided so greatly in the work of the restoration.

*299. What are the three pairs in the prophets?*

The two prophets sent to Nineveh—Jonah and Nahum; the two prophets of the captivity—Ezekiel and Daniel; the two adulterous women in Ezekiel, who are types of the spiritual unfaithfulness of Samaria and Jerusalem—Aholah and Aholiab.

*300. What are the seven leading pairs of the gospels?*

The father and mother of John the Baptizer—Zechariah and Elisabeth; the mother of our Lord and her husband—Mary and Joseph; the two persons mentioned as being present in the temple at the presentation of the child JESUS—Simeon and Anna; the two heavenly visitants at the transfiguration of JESUS—Moses and Elijah; the two friends of the crucified Saviour—Joseph of Arimathea and Nicodemus; the two women who were last at the cross and first at the sepulchre—Mary Magdalene and Mary the mother of James; the two of the twelve who ran to the sepulchre—Peter and John.

*301. Who were the two pairs of brothers among the twelve apostles?*

Peter and Andrew, the sons of Jonas; James and John, the sons of Zebedee.

*302. What are the nine leading pairs in the Acts?*

The two candidates for the place in the apostolic college made vacant by the defection and death of Judas—Joseph-Justus and Matthias, the latter of whom was chosen; the two leading apostles at Pentecost—Peter and John; the two leading apostles in the history in the Acts—Peter and Paul; the two persons punished by death for lying and hypocrisy—Ananias and Sapphira; the first two foreign missionaries—Paul and Barnabas; Paul's two converts at Athens—Dionysius and Damaris; the two governors before whom Paul was arraigned—Felix and Festus; the first two Christian martyrs—Stephen the deacon and James the apostle; the two Roman captains into whose hands Paul fell—Lysias and

Julius; the two persons raised from the dead—Dorcas (by Peter at Joppa) and Eutychus (by Paul at Troy).

*303. What are the four pairs of Paul?*

His two warm friends and helpers—Aquila and his wife Priscilla; the two disciples he ordained as ministers—Timothy and Titus; the two blasphemers he delivered to Satan —Hymeneus and Alexander; the two prominent men who turned away from him in Asia Minor—Phygellus and Hermogenes.

*304. What are four great trinities in the Bible?*

The three great subjects of the Bible—God, man, redemption; its three great advents—that of Adam upon earth, that of CHRIST for salvation, and the coming of CHRIST to judgment; the three chief Christian graces—faith, hope, love; the trinity of trinities—Father, Son, and Holy Spirit.

*305. What are the three great eras of the world's history?*

The Patriarchal, the Mosaic, and the Christian eras.

*306. What are the three great periods in the Jewish national history?*

The theocracy (from Moses to the monarchy), the monarchy, and the restoration.

*307. What is the division of the threefold historical books which cover the national history of the Jews?*

The period of the theocracy— Joshua, Judges, and Ruth; the period of the monarchy—the three doubles—the Samuels, the Kings, and the Chronicles; the period of the restoration—Ezra, Nehemiah, and Esther.

*308. What is the threefold division of the prophets?*

The pre-exile prophets, the prophets of the captivity, and the prophets of the restoration.

*309. What are the six leading trinities in Genesis?*

In the creation story—God, nature, and man; the three sons of Adam—Cain, Abel, and Seth; the three sons of Noah—Shem, Ham, and Japheth; the three sons of Zerah —Abraham, Nahor, and Haran; the three great ancestors of the Hebrew people—Abraham, Isaac, and Jacob; the first three great Oriental empires—Egypt, Chaldea, and Assyria.

*310. What are the trinities in Exodus?*

The three divisions of the book itself—Israel in Egypt, from Egypt to Sinai, and the transactions at Sinai; the three principal events at Sinai—the giving of the law, the lapse and restoration of the people, and the erection of the tabernacle.

*311. What triplet is mentioned in Leviticus?*

The three great annual festivals of the Jews—the Passover, Pentecost, and the feast of Tabernacles—the Harvest Home of the Hebrew people.

*312. What are the three triplets in Numbers?*

The three leading subjects of the book itself—the camp, the march toward Canaan, and the forty years in the wilderness; the three rebels—Korah, Dathan, and Abiram, whom the earth swallowed; the three mountains mentioned in connection with the history—Sinai, whence the people started on their march to Canaan, Hor, where Aaron died, and Nebo (Pisgah), where the decease of Moses took place.

*313. What are the three great pentateuchal prophecies respecting CHRIST?*

The protevangelium in Genesis (3 : 15); the star and sceptre prophecy of Balaam in Numbers (24 : 17); and the prediction of Moses in Deuteronomy (18 : 15) that a great prophet like unto himself should appear amongst the people.

*314. What are the two triplets in Joshua?*

The three cities of refuge on the east side of Jordan—Bezer in the wilderness, Ramoth in Gilead, and Golan in Bashan; and the three on the west side—Hebron in Judah, Shechem in Ephraim, and Kedesh in Galilee.

*315. What are the five trinities in the monarchical books?*

The three doubles themselves—the Samuels, the Kings, and the Chronicles; the three sovereigns of the united kingdom—Saul, David, and Solomon; the three sons of Zeruiah who were too much for King David—Joab, Abishai, and Asahel; King David's threefold choice as a punishment for his sin in numbering the people—famine, defeat, pestilence; the three captive kings of Judah—Jehoiakim, Jehoiachin, and Zedekiah.

*316. What are the trinities of the restoration era?*

The three books which treat of the era itself—Ezra, Nehemiah, and Esther; the three leading men in the restoration—Zerubbabel, Ezra, and Nehemiah; the three prophets of the restoration—Haggai, Zechariah, and Malachi; the three obstructionists in Nehemiah—Sanballat the Horonite, Tobiah the Ammonite, and Geshem the Arabian.

*317. What are the trinities in Job?*

The patriarch's three friends—Eliphaz the Temanite, Bildad the Shuhite, and Zophar the Naamathite; the three animals in Job—the Arabian war-horse, the behemoth, and the leviathan; Job's three daughters, born to him after his affliction—Jemima, Kezia, and Karen-happuch.

*318. What are the names of the three Hebrew prophetesses?*

Miriam, Deborah, and Huldah.

*319. What three children of the prophet Hosea had their names given to them by God Himself?*

Jezreel, Lo-ruhamah, and Lo-ammi.

*320. What three persons were raised from the dead in the Old Testament?*

The son of the widow of Zarephath (by Elijah), that of the Shunammite woman (by Elisha), and the man who revived and stood upon his feet when he was let down into the sepulchre of Elisha and touched the bones of the prophet.

*321. What three persons did our Lord raise from·the dead?*

Jairus' daughter, the son of the widow of Nain, and His friend Lazarus, the brother of Martha and Mary.

*322. Who, besides the prophet himself, were the three heroes in Daniel?*

Shadrach, Meshach, and Abednego, who were cast into the burning fiery furnace because they refused to worship the golden image which Nebuchadnezzar the king had set up.

*323. Who were the three children besides JESUS whose names were alike foretold?*

Isaac, Ishmael, and John the Baptizer.

*324. Which are the three synoptic gospels?*

Matthew, Mark, and Luke.

*325. What are three important scenes in the early life of JESUS?*

His flight into Egypt, His presentation in the temple, and His appearance among the doctors.

*326. Who were the three favorite disciples of JESUS?*

Peter, James, and John.

*327. What were the three most dramatic scenes in the life of JESUS?*

His transfiguration, His crucifixion, and His ascension.

*328. What were the three principal sects among the Jews in the time of CHRIST?*

The Pharisees, the Sadducees, and the Herodians.

*329. Who are the three leading characters in the Acts whose names begin with P?*

Peter the preacher, Philip the evangelist, and Paul the missionary—Peter, Philip, and Paul.

*330. What are three marked periods in the life of the apostle Paul?*

His persecution *of* CHRIST, his conversion *to* CHRIST, and his labors and sufferings *for* CHRIST.

*331. What were the three most exciting episodes in the life of the apostle Paul?*

His address to the Athenians on Mars' Hill, his address to the excited Jews from the steps of the castle of Antonia at Jerusalem, and his address before Agrippa in his own defence.

*332. What were the three capitals associated with the Apostolic Church?*

Jerusalem, Antioch in Syria, and Ephesus in Asia Minor.

*333. Who are three military men mentioned in the Acts?*

Cornelius, Lysias, and Julius—Roman centurions.

*334. Who are the three most famous women of the Apostolic Church?*

Dorcas, a woman of Joppa, full of good words and alms-deeds which she did, and whom the apostle Peter raised from the dead; Phebe, who was a servant of the church which was at Cenchrea; and Priscilla, who was a helper of the apostle Paul.

*335. What are the five trinities of the apostle Paul?*

His threefold benediction—grace, mercy, and peace; his three chief graces—faith, hope, and charity; his three parts of human personality—body, soul, and spirit; this three deserters—Phygellus, Hermogenes, and Demas; his three opposers—Demetrius the silversmith, Alexander the coppersmith, and Satan the great adversary.

*336. What are the trinities in James?*

The three steps to ruin—lust, sin, death; the three attributes of worldly wisdom—earthly, sensual, devilish.

*337. What were the three political divisions of the Holy Land in the time of CHRIST?*

Judea, Samaria, and Galilee—the southern, central, and northern division.

*338. What were the three cities of JESUS?*

Bethlehem, where He was born; Nazareth, where He was brought up; and Capernaum, where most of His mighty works were done.

THE

# BIBLE CATECHIST

AN INSTRUCTION

IN

## BIBLICAL INTRODUCTION FOR THE YOUNG

BY THE

REV. W. H. GILL, D.D.

AUTHOR OF "THE TEMPLE OPENED"

———•———

PHILADELPHIA

PRESBYTERIAN BOARD OF PUBLICATION
AND SABBATH-SCHOOL WORK

No. 1334 CHESTNUT STREET